In memory, honor, and gratefulness to my parents for all they have shared with me.

THIS SIGN WAS MINE

Message Received!

PATTI RAE FLETCHER

BALBOA.
PRESS

A DIVISION OF HAY HOUSE

Balboa Press books may be ordered through booksellers or by contacting:

Balboa Press
A Division of Hay House
1663 Liberty Drive
Bloomington, IN 47403
www.balboapress.com
1 (877) 407-4847

Because of the dynamic nature of the Internet, any web addresses or
links contained in this book may have changed since publication and
may no longer be valid. The views expressed in this work are solely those
of the author and do not necessarily reflect the views of the publisher,
and the publisher hereby disclaims any responsibility for them.

The author of this book does not dispense medical advice or prescribe the use
of any technique as a form of treatment for physical, emotional, or medical
problems without the advice of a physician, either directly or indirectly. The
intent of the author is only to offer information of a general nature to help
you in your quest for emotional and spiritual well-being. In the event you use
any of the information in this book for yourself, which is your constitutional
right, the author and the publisher assume no responsibility for your actions.

Any people depicted in stock imagery provided by Thinkstock are models,
and such images are being used for illustrative purposes only.
Certain stock imagery © Thinkstock.

Print information available on the last page.

ISBN: 978-1-5043-3625-3 (sc)
ISBN: 978-1-5043-3627-7 (hc)
ISBN: 978-1-5043-3626-0 (e)

Library of Congress Control Number: 2015910680

Balboa Press rev. date: 07/29/2015

Contents

Acknowledgements

My deep appreciation goes out to all those who took time from their busy schedules to do a critique on this work. Thank You!

To my friends and family who have shown their support in many ways. I love you.

To Balboa Press and all of your teams, I'm impressed with your personal consistent friendliness, professionalism, and most of all, for all that you have taught me along this extraordinary journey. Thank you!

My heartfelt gratefulness goes first to my husband for his love, support, and always being there for me, no matter what I'm going through or what dream I'm pursuing.

Introduction

Over the past few years, signs, synchronicities, bizarre happenings, or divine interventions, however you name them, have become powerful in my life and have forced me to take notice and claim *This Sign Was Mine*!

I now understand that at times those crazy instances hold a much-needed message. I feel these signs are meant to inform, comfort, and help us along destiny's path, whether it's an adversity in our life or a goal. My signs have appeared in several forms—as images, sensations, rings, hearts, doves, people, and actual road signs.

This book came about as I tried to figure out the why(s) of my life, my purpose, my feelings, my doubts, and why things happen the way they do. Many episodes have happened in my life that I didn't understand as I'm sure everyone can relate. I've felt confused, empty, and lost. So I did what I've done for years and wrote them down. I began with the first monumental event with which I connected—the one that blew me away and had me asking,

"Is this a miracle?" This particular incident, which you'll read about in chapter 1, made me realize there is much more. There is something powerful, something I had no control over whatsoever, and it brought me back from a desperate, dark place.

I've been gifted with images and sensations that have changed my life. The messages have been clear; they've brought hope, confidence, and an inner peace during even the worst of circumstances. They've also helped me discover my dreams. Because of these signs, I've grown in faith and have never had more confidence in making the correct life decisions.

Each chapter in this book is an individual story where universal signs have presented themselves to me in unlikely ways, and in some unusual places.

My wish for you, the reader, is that you will have a renewed awareness and not brush off coincidence. I feel in my soul that everything happens for a reason. My hope is that you will give any strange occurrence some deep thought with an open mind and heart and keep moving forward. I believe if you pay attention you will soon recognize and welcome your own signs and their messages. I feel it's possible that you too will receive answers to some of life's difficult questions, struggles, and guidance for your own hopes and dreams as well.

CHAPTER 1

My Rings of Life

I have lived on the lip of insanity, wanting to know reasons, knocking on a door. It opens. I've been knocking from the inside!
—Rumi

1977–2005 (This synchronicity began more than thirty years ago and built its way to the perfect life-changing moment.)

A rush of air filled my lungs, and I was unable to move, unable to breathe. My jaw hung open for several seconds before the high-pitched scream reverberated through the house, almost scaring my youngest son to death. By the time he made it to my bedroom, I (his forty-something-year-old mother) was jumping on the bed, red-faced like a two-year-old. Both fists squeezed tight and pumped in the air, first one and then the other. Hysterical laughter and tears of joy flowed from my face.

It All Began

On my seventeenth birthday, I received a jewelry box, a proper one. It was made from fine wood, not plastic. No cartoon characters were on it anywhere. I gushed and fell in love with the elegant box and the handsome man with a heartthrob smile who gave it to me.

The fresh-cut wood scent mingled with the dark walnut stain. I ran my fingers over the detailed curved surfaces, stopping at the etched-glass windows that allowed a peek inside. I couldn't imagine ever having enough jewelry to fill all of the compartments. My favorite area was the unique pull-down drawer, which was slotted and lined with plush gold velvet to hug each ring. The rows were set at an angle like theater seats.

1977: When I received the brochure that advertised high school graduation rings for sale, my mom shared my excitement, knowing my love of rings. Dad said it was darned expensive at $300 but agreed to buy it for me since I was an honor student.

The multicut, gorgeous aquamarine was nestled within the antiqued gold setting and embossed with my graduation year. I wore it with pride for approximately one month.

One morning before school, I went to put on my ring and gasped when it wasn't in my jewelry box. I tried not to panic. I took a deep breath and did what I was taught to do all my life: retrace the last moments I remembered wearing or seeing the missing item. I envisioned it to be at school. I remembered taking it off to wash my hands: the bell rang, and I must have rushed off and left it on the bathroom sink. I checked the lost and found first thing that day and each day after for over a month without success. The office secretary promised to call if it was ever returned.

Prior to losing my graduation ring, I'd lost two birthstone rings, one from my parents and the other from my boyfriend. One was a bit loose even with the yarn wrapped around the band. I believed I'd lost it while swimming in a lake up north. I couldn't quite figure out when the other went missing.

1980: When I got married I never took my wedding band off, well aware of my previous luck with rings.

For our third wedding anniversary, I received a lovely ring from my husband. This one glistened with diamonds. It took my breath away.

We had planned a camping trip for our one-week vacation that year. Two of my favorite things are fishing and hiking. This wouldn't be a good time to wear my anniversary ring. Nope—diamonds, worm guts, and fish scales weren't a good mix.

The evening before we left on vacation, my husband worked a night shift. In that semigroggy sleep right before I dozed off, always a bit wary of being alone anyway, my last thought was about robberies and where to hide my anniversary ring while we were away. My intention was to hide it somewhere clever, somewhere besides my jewelry box, where a burglar would find it for sure. I'd place the ring in a jacket pocket in my closet when I got up the next morning. I felt proud of that plan as I fell asleep. My husband came in from work early and was anxious to get the car packed and get on the road. I never gave the ring another thought. It was a fabulous, fun trip.

Several weeks later, we had a wedding to attend. While I dressed for the event, the sparkle of my necklace reminded me of how well the diamond ring would match. When I opened the ring section of the jewelry box, the ring wasn't there. I gasped, *Oh no!* I was certain I'd put it in there. My mind raced to the point of when I'd worn it last. *I won't tell my husband; it'll turn up. It has to. Oh my God, not another lost ring! My husband will kill me; well, maybe not kill me, but he will be furious for sure.*

When we first arrived at the wedding, my eyes traveled to my empty right ring finger. It was when the bride and her father walked down the aisle, one arm linked with his daughter and the other at his pocket. *The pocket. Oh yeah, I'd hidden the ring in the pocket of my jacket in the closet.* I squeezed my husband's hand as the vows were being said and relaxed at last, grateful for him and for the jacket memory.

4

The next morning I thumbed through the hangers in search of the jacket to retrieve my hidden ring. A slice of ice raced down my spine. Tears filled my eyes with the realization I'd taken that jacket along with others to a resale consignment shop the previous month. I rushed to the store, and, of course, it was Sunday, and the store was closed.

The next day I returned to the store. I spotted the rack with jackets and searched for mine. It wasn't there. In choked breaths I explained what had happened. The clerk was sympathetic. It was a cash-only shop. She told me they didn't keep any records on people who purchased items, and no one had returned a diamond ring to the store. She was very sorry and took my number in case the ring ever showed up.

When I finally confessed this to my husband, he reacted as I had expected, and I didn't blame him one bit. In his shoes I would've felt the same way. He said he wouldn't buy me any more jewelry from that day on. He couldn't be any angrier at me than I was at myself though. I was outraged at my irresponsibility and lost a bit more of my confidence.

Years went by as I prayed my anniversary ring would show up someday. That never happened. I remained angry with myself, so I changed my prayer to, *whoever found my ring, please let it be someone in need.* I'd try to envision a person who pawned it for cash to clothe and feed her hungry family. That helped me finally forgive myself and *almost* let it go.

The years had flown. I now had two strong-willed sons. Their teenage years were upon us, and they weren't going very well. Some bad choices by our children caused much heartache during the same time my dad had suffered a massive heart attack. He'd been in intensive care for fifty-seven days, on and off life support. The doctors turned to me, an only child, for all the answers and decisions about Dad, even though my mom sat next me. One day I noticed on Dad's chart there was a handwritten, highlighted note at the top: "Wife/Dementia? Talk to daughter."

I explained that Mom was fine, just tired most of the time and slow to speak but comprehended things well. To my knowledge, she didn't have dementia.

The stress built until I couldn't talk to anyone about anything without a sharp tone or tears. This caused my husband and me to grow distant. He held his feelings in, not wanting to burden me more. We spoke to each other through Post-it notes on the kitchen counter, as we were on different schedules. The weeks progressed into months; each day we thought and were told it would be Dad's last. We went about trying to fix things as best we could, but most of it was out of our control. My husband took care of everything at home, and I took Mom to the hospital every day to be with Dad as many hours as they would allow us to stay.

I felt the lowest I'd ever felt, to the point of knowing there was no reason for me to be alive. My life didn't matter because no matter what I'd said or done, it wasn't going to get better. Dad was expected to die at any moment. Mom would get worse and probably have to be institutionalized. The boys couldn't seem to do anything right and weren't listening to us, and my husband was overwhelmed with doing his best to deal with work, me, the kids, and two households—ours, and Mom and Dad's. He still found the time to relieve me from Dad's bedside at the hospital. The aloneness consumed me. Mom barely spoke a word all those days. I talked but didn't really know if she understood what was going on or what I was saying. No one had the answers. I couldn't and didn't make a bit of difference. Things seemed to get worse every day. I was exhausted.

With my nerves being what they were, my hands broke out in itchy hives one day and began to swell. I oiled my finger to get my wedding band off and placed it in the ring compartment of my jewelry box until my hands healed. When I closed the ring drawer and turned to walk away, I heard something, a soft clink. I turned back and reopened the drawer; the wedding ring was gone. I slid my hand beneath the box. Nothing was there but dust. I tried to take the empty ring compartment out, but it was hinged at the bottom, so I removed the drawer above and squeezed my hand into the tiny opening. I shoved until the tips of my fingers touched something near the floor of the box—cool metal.

I wiggled my fingers lower and was able to pinch them close enough together to bring up a single ring. I reached in again and again and brought out the diamond anniversary ring, my high school graduation ring, a gold pinky ring, three birthstone rings, and others I had totally forgotten about over the decades. Twelve! Twelve rings I'd over many years convinced myself that I had lost.

My tears turned into uncontrollable joyful sobs as I settled on the bed after my bouncing frolic. I opened both hands to show my wide-eyed son my treasures. With a shake of his head, an eye roll, and a chuckle, he said, "Mom, really, is that all? It's a bunch of rings. What are you bawling for?" Being a teenager, he walked away probably thinking his weird mother had finally lost her mind.

I, to this day, wear those once lost rings on every finger and presently only one thumb, never removing them. Someday I'll find the right ring for my other thumb. I've tried on many shopping excursions, and even bought a few. None have ever felt or fit right. Mom said many times while we shopped, "It's because the right one hasn't come along yet. It will, and you'll know it when it does!"

This gift, the finding of all these rings after all these decades, was a significant sign that presented itself to me at the precise moment when I had given up all hope on myself and on everyone I loved.

This single event bears the question, Why hadn't I heard that *tink* before? It had been happening for over three decades. That jewelry box had pulled rings from their velvet seats and deposited them to the bottom behind the drawer since I'd lived at home with my parents. Was I really that unaware? Maybe they didn't make a sound until the very day I needed to find them. Did the universe somehow know I would need something gigantic to convince me there was hope in the future? My future, when everything in my life was torn apart and when all I could think was nothing I'd ever done or said mattered to anyone, so there was no reason for me to be here.

Now, every time a gemstone catches the sun or twists on my finger, I slide it around and remember why each ring is there. Its message still clear in my mind, it serves as a reminder of the person I used to be and how much I've grown, but, most of all, each ring gives me hope in any and all situations—especially at those times when I think there is none.

This sign was mine!

Miraculous things happened soon after that day.

Dad survived those near-death days in the hospital. The doctors took a chance by putting a pacemaker in him not knowing if he was strong enough to make it through the procedure. In recovery, his eyes shined with a confident *I'm back* kind of look. He lived a quality life for another decade.

Mom didn't have dementia at all. It was a case of being overmedicated, and she returned to her normal joking self once she changed doctors and medications.

Both our sons learned some life lessons the hard way and grew up to be fine young successful gentlemen. I'm so proud of them.

My husband and I have been married over thirty-five years, and he often buys me jewelry, even rings now. I have acquired a second jewelry box to fill, one with a ring drawer that is properly positioned and doesn't steal my precious gems.

I am consumed with hope, gratefulness, and love and understand now why it is so important to never ever give up.

CHAPTER 2

Right Place, Right Time?

Only through experience of trial and suffering can the soul be strengthened, vision cleared, ambition inspired, and success achieved. —Helen Keller

2006

My college course writing instructor had said my article about a strip canoe was like "a prayer in wood," and wouldn't take long to sell. My critique group helped me tighten this article to what they called absolute perfection. I had revised this work so many times, I had it memorized. Then I had sent it out to many different magazines and received rejection upon rejection. What was I doing wrong?

While I was having a personal pity party one evening after receiving my ninth rejection, I came across an outdoor magazine on the Internet inviting its readers to submit their stories. I thought, *Why not? It can't hurt.* I took a deep breath, raised my eyes to the heavens, and hit the send key. My article materialized somewhere in Iowa in some editor's mailbox. I wondered how long I would have to wait for this rejection and then slouched into my chair with a heavy sigh and sipped on my wine.

Maybe I need to be done, terminado, fini! I banged on the desk, threw up my arms, and said, "Just give me a sign if you want me to continue on this writing rollercoaster!" I didn't know what to do. The rejection letters hurt, even though any writer knows we aren't supposed to take rejection personally, writing is personal, therefore difficult not to take it that way.

As much as I felt in my heart I was meant to write, and I adore weaving words together in my own unique way, maybe this writing gig wasn't for me after all.

As it turned out, I was wrong. There was a ding indicating an e-mail had arrived before I even left my desk chair. This certain editor was having a late night also and had read my submission, and then wrote back within minutes. It was after midnight here. In his response, he referred to me as a freelance writer (that was the first time anyone had honored me with that title) and wanted to know a quote on the canoe article I had sent right then. He went on to say he wanted to see whatever I write first before I send my submissions to any other publications. I sat in shock for a long while in utter disbelief.

As Bill Engvall an American standup comedian and actor often says, "And here's your sign." I wrote many articles for this editor and his magazine over the course of several years. My passion for writing grew stronger and to more determined levels to the point it had me thinking that maybe someday, even though the thought terrified me at the time, I may attempt to write a book.

Because of this editor's belief in my writing, I didn't give up that night as I had all intentions of doing. I have one middle school camping novel finished, and it's in the process of being submitted to editors, along with over two dozen publications in a variety of magazines.

Thank you to that late-night editor for making a difference in my life. Being in the right place at the right moment can change your thinking and therefore change lives. It changed mine.

This sign was mine.

Ask and it will be given to you; seek and you will find; knock and the door will be opened to you—Matthew 7:7

CHAPTER 3

Recognition

If the original plan doesn't go as expected, there's a reason.
Release it, and make room for destiny. —P. R. Fletcher

1992: When my children began elementary school, I decided to help in the library. After three years of volunteer work a couple of hours a week, I was asked if I had any interest in a part-time position that would be available soon and to please submit an application. The students already knew me, and I had a good handle on the job that needed to be done. Employment was never my intention. I was a stay-at-home mom who decorated cakes to bring in extra income. I enjoyed being a homemaker, a mom, and a volunteer, but I had also grown to love the students, the library, and the awesome feeling of being surrounded by books. It felt like a tailored fit.

Both my husband and I were uncertain about taking on more with two young boys at the time, but with the encouragement of the enthusiastic principal Jane, and Marie, the fabulous person I helped in the library, I became employed through our city's school district as a part-time media technologist. I job shared with Marie, who was taking classes toward her teaching certificate and needed two days off each week for her college studies in 1995.

Fast Forward to 2010

It was the last staff meeting of the school year. I had received a congratulatory pin from my employer in the morning for fifteen years of service, with much praise. This didn't include the three volunteer years. By the end of that same day I was told my job position was being eliminated, and all the media techs in the district were being laid off, six in all. I was devastated. I had lost the job that I had loved and served with passion and dedication for all of those years and could only wonder why. Everything happens for a reason, right? I tried to convince myself, even though it didn't make much sense at that time.

I couldn't imagine finding a new job that I loved as much as this past one. I made the decision that maybe I'd pursue my writing interest and see if I could make it more than a hobby. I'd had publishing successes, and the writing institutes' instructors pushed for me take a more advanced study, a course on writing and marketing books for children.

I decided to take my third course and put off the employment search for the time being.

Mom encouraged me to stay on the writing path and was my biggest fan, no matter what I wrote. Unexpectedly, five months after my job loss, she passed away. I'm so grateful for all those extra moments I spent with her. As a result of her death, my father's health declined quickly, and he needed my everyday attention and care. I happened to be available and didn't have to go through the additional stress of missing work or the decision of giving up the job that I loved to help him. I could continue my online writing course from home, mine or his when needed, without disrupting his care.

Two life-changing occurrences came from having the media technologist job that I was in the beginning so uncertain about and its devastating lay-off at the end.

First, it was during my time in this elementary school library that I discovered my strong attraction to children's literature. I loved when the students would gasp as I ended a page and would urge me to read more, or would attempt to hide their emotion at sad parts. My favorite was when they would laugh out loud. I felt like I made a difference when students asked about authors or mentioned characters from a story I had read to them during their library time.

But it was the poorly written books, the ones that couldn't hold a child's attention for five minutes, let alone for a half hour while I read aloud. Those books angered me and made me wonder why they were in the library at all. Often when I came home, I'd complain to my husband of how I had read through several books before I found one that I felt would entice or inspire students to become literature lovers and lifelong readers: which was always my goal. I grumbled often, "I could write better books."

My husband was the one who finally asked, after he listened to my weekly complaints, "Well, why don't you write one then, and quit talking about it?"

I said, "Right," and shook my head, "I've never written anything, except letters to relatives and maybe a few politicians. I wouldn't know where to begin anyway."

My husband's question ignited the spark of wonder deep within myself and raised my own question of how to write a book. *Maybe someday, I'll look into it.*

Not long after this seed was planted, I thumbed through a magazine at the dentist office. I ran across a full-page ad for the Institute of Children's Literature, and there it was in large bold letters across the middle of the magazine asking if I wanted to learn to write a children's book. Below the words was a number for one-on-one instruction, college credits, and home study courses. I asked the dental receptionist if she would copy the page for me. She did, and from that point, my life forever changed.

Second, this layoff gave me extra, and the much treasured, time to be with my mom and then time to care for Dad as his health declined.

The timing of the job loss was impeccable for what was to come and what was meant to be on my destiny's path. I began my writing studies six years before the layoff and never dreamed it would turn into a second career.

Looking back throughout my life, I realized there were many coincidences before I recognized them as my personal life signs. I was too busy and brushed them off never giving them another thought.

I make a continuous effort to be more aware and to accept whatever signs are gifted to me, whether the signs are troubled or terrific. I'm now convinced there is always a reason to, let go, move on, and be ready to welcome whatever is coming next on my journey.

This sign was mine!

CHAPTER 4

The Love Chip

You have to accept whatever comes and the only important thing is that you meet it with courage and with the best that you have to give. —Eleanor Roosevelt

December 2013

The hospital staff was determined to get Dad home for Christmas Day. In order for that to happen, they would have to give me a quick lesson on how to take care of the catheter that couldn't be removed as of yet. Once this was explained, Dad, still so weak from the congestive heart failure, said yes in a barely audible voice to going home and having me do his private catheter care.

On Christmas Eve, my husband, in his bright yellow pickup, arrived at the entrance of the hospital to take his father-in-law home. He had done this over a dozen times in the past couple of years. Dad teased my husband about his shocking yellow truck but commented often of how much he loved riding in it and seeing it come around the corner. The home-care nurse would begin visits the day after Christmas; until then I had to figure things out on my own.

This was the turning point, when I moved in with Dad and went from semicaregiver to a total caregiver. I thought it would be for a couple of weeks, as in the past. I was wrong. Soon, to my realization, over a month had gone by, and I was no longer thought of or treated as a daughter. I seemed to be everything but a daughter to my dad—nurse, secretary, maid, waitress, therapist, chauffeur, and cook. My heart ached for the tenderness that I had always known from Dad, and now, so unlike him, there was only silence and irritation.

I missed Mom and wanted to ask her so many questions. We loved our girls' gang up on Dad moments through my childhood years. "What are we going to do with him?" we'd both say and laugh at the same time. But most of all, I missed Dad's slow-motion smile. I missed all the living room dance parties. Patsy Cline, Elvis, Boots Randolph, and Al Hirt rocked our house for many years. My parents loved to dance and couldn't afford to go out, so the living room became their dance floor.

These days Dad's voice was a strained whisper, and his appetite dwindled. Anyone who knew my dad knew he loved to eat and there wasn't much he'd refuse. With eleven siblings growing up, he'd often tell people, "You learn to appreciate food." He savored his meals, consumed large portions, and always ate slowly. He often moaned from pure enjoyment during and after bites, and always cleaned his plate. When he quit eating, reality kicked in, and I knew things had worsened.

He slept in the chair most of the day and was in bed by ten every night.

"Dad, is your stomach upset? Are you in any pain?" I asked often.

"No, just tired," he'd grumble without opening his eyes and sometimes not bother to answer. He often pretended to be asleep.

I felt helpless. So helpless I decided I would bring him a plate of his favorite forbidden food. Anything had to be better than eating nothing, right? From the snack closet, I rustled a bag of chips, in hopes he would open his eyes. He didn't.

I poured a pile of his favorite snack on a paper plate and said, "Dad, have some chips, they are good and fresh." He waved me away. My eyes flooded with tears as they so often did these days. I grabbed a handful for myself and put them on a napkin. I left the plate for him next to his chair. I took mine to the kitchen table to work on a Bible study I had begun several weeks ago, leaving Dad to his pretend sleep.

The tears stopped when I noticed there on the top of my pile was a chip with a brown spot, a hole in its center. I almost threw it away and then took a closer look. That hole formed a shape, the shape of a tiny heart, a bit burned and ragged around the edges, and my first thought was, *a heart that felt like mine.*

Hearts happen to be my favorite shape since I was a small child. It was one of the first things I learned how to draw, and to this day I still doodle heart shapes whenever I have a pencil in my hand. Hearts are the perfect symbol of love. But this heart, in the center of this potato chip at this moment was more than any doodle. As tears once again filled my eyes and streamed over my cheeks, a distinct thought so vivid it caused the top of my head to tingle was, *Why in the heck am I crying over a potato chip?* Then my brain transformed into a newsreel and in bold block letters sent me the answer. *Why hadn't I thought of it before? Why didn't I know?* Suddenly I did, I knew. It was a reminder of Dad's unconditional love for me, something I needed never to forget.

Dads disconnect from me as a daughter was the only way he could cope with the humiliation of all I had to do for him. All the things he, an independent, strong man, was not capable of doing for himself any longer. A quiet calm and understanding ran through my body, stealing away my sadness about the situation, and eased me into a relaxed state of being.

The sensation was like nothing I'd ever felt before. The only way I can describe the feeling is that it had that cozy warmth of a cup of hot chocolate after playing along while in the snow, except this cup was filled with complete love and understanding, and it at that moment consumed me, giving me the confidence I needed to have to know we'd get through this.

That chip was meant for me and was perfectly timed, carrying a much-needed message!

This sign was mine.

I had no clue that this heart sign was the first of many to come. Rarely a day goes by that I don't see a heart somewhere and sometimes in the most unusual places.

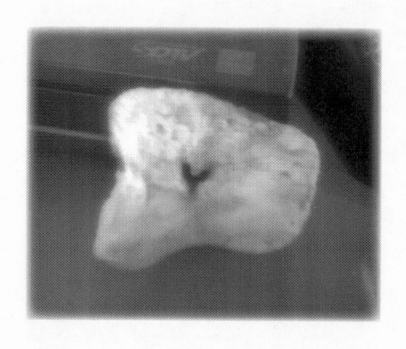

CHAPTER 5

Bible Study

During this difficult time, these words caressed and calmed me as an ancient lullaby of awareness. —P. R. Fletcher

Winter 2013

Dad had yet another terrible bout of congestive heart failure, more blood transfusions, and another ten-day stay in the hospital. One doctor recommended hospice. Dad wouldn't hear any of that talk. This episode was worse than the last one. It zapped what little strength he had left. He grew weaker with each passing day.

Once at home again, we had the usual social workers, home-care nurses, occupational therapists, and physical therapist; even the foot doctor was coming to the house, because Dad's legs were now too weak and unsteady to manipulate the two landing steps to go out the door to any appointments.

He slept later and later, causing me to check on him to make sure his chest still moved with life. One of my worst fears happened late one morning while I was in the kitchen waiting for Dad to awake, wondering if I could talk him into eating an egg.

I heard a loud thud and his weak groan. He'd stood up too quick and had tried to make it to the bathroom. (His walker was at the end of the bed.) He had taken a few steps before his legs collapsed, and he slid down the wall. I wanted to call the ambulance, but he insisted he was fine.

My efforts were futile for lifting Dad even though he weighed less than me now; no matter what I tried, I wasn't strong enough. His upper body strength was depleted and he couldn't help, not even to scoot. He wasn't bleeding from anywhere; I could see no bumps or bruises. I leaned a pillow next to the dresser and made him as comfortable as I could. The physical therapist was due at the house any minute. I sat cross-legged on the floor in front of Dad and worked on the grocery list. I mentioned a menu for our evening meal while his only input was a shrug.

After Dad's fall, and the fact that I couldn't maneuver him back into the bed or chair alone, was when my sleep problems worsened. I lived in a constant state of worry, but now it was worse with little or no sleep.

What if he got up during the night and fell again, and I didn't hear him? What if he called out, and I was in a deep sleep? And, I couldn't even contemplate what if he didn't wake up at all in the morning?

I lay awake each night and listened to the now unfamiliar sounds of my childhood home and neighborhood. I struggled to hear Dad breathe with the recent arrival of an oxygen unit that hummed through the night. I missed Mom, and I missed living with my husband.

As Dad grew more physically unstable, more fear and depression seeped in. I believe this is when the true reality of losing Dad came into perspective. I was petrified. How could I go on with both my parents gone? There wasn't anything else the doctors could do. I knew it, and Dad knew it too. They couldn't fix him anymore with surgeries, therapies, blood transfusions, pacemakers, or medication changes as they had over the past years.

I did my best to put on the fake it till you make it smile every day, but each day a bit of me died right along with Dad. I felt alone, and the burden was heavier than anything I had ever carried. Nobody could do anything—not me, not the doctors, not friends or family. There was no rest in my mind, heart, or soul until … I changed the time of day that I worked on that Bible study.

An important person came into my life over a decade ago. I met Maggie at a writers' conference, and we've stayed in touch over the years. I believe people come into and go out of our lives for certain reasons, and I think this Bible study was an important one, but certainly not the only reason she came into my life.

Maggie sent me an email that mentioned a Bible study she was going to join online, and asked if I would be interested in participating also. She said, "I thought of you. This study is geared toward Christian women who feel or have felt alone, hopeless, helpless, and overwhelmed with life's burdens."

Hmm, I thought, I could relate to all those things, but I didn't feel up to doing anything. I was emotionally and physically exhausted and didn't think I was willing or even able to commit to something for six weeks. *It couldn't help my issues anyway; they weren't going away, so why bother?* I had never done a Bible study before and had no idea of how to do one or what kind of time was required.

Maggie had planted the seed, and it took root whether I wanted it to or not.

Since Dad slept so much now, and my sleep was sporadic at best, I had free time. Afraid to leave Dad alone too long, I only left his house when I had to do an errand or when my husband would stop by after work. I decided, okay; why not give the Bible study a try? I could do it in-between Dad's naps and therapist visits.

Once I began doing this study in the evenings after Dad was in bed, instead of trying to steal moments during the day, I felt my body start to relax as I read the assigned verses and found the answers to the author's questions in the workbook.

My focus was clearer without the day's interruptions. This made all the difference. The all-alone feeling disappeared. The stories in the study were a reminder that other people had gone through worse and survived, in the Bible and out. My sleep deepened and I felt refreshed in the mornings. I woke ready to take on another day and fulfill all of my dad's needs with a gratefulness I hadn't felt in a long while.

God knew I wouldn't have paid for this study. He also knew I wouldn't leave my dad in the evenings to meet at a church or any other location. It just so happened that this study was offered for the first time online, and even the workbook was sent free with registration. What great timing!

I've never heard scripture attached to real-life circumstances with so much love. The author shared her intimate trials and how she survived them in this Bible study. Her generosity, love, and kindness came into my life at this much-needed time and will never be forgotten.

"At times our own light goes out and is rekindled by a spark from another person. Each of us has cause to think with deep gratitude of those who have lighted the flame within us."—Albert Schweitzer

I'm forever grateful to my friend Maggie for the invite to take this study with her, introducing me through the Internet to her friend who writes fabulous Bible studies, but most of all for rekindling my spark.

I hadn't been inspired or done any writing except for course assignments for the past year. But in the midst of this study I felt inspired to write a poem. It came to me one night after reading the two verses below.

Isaiah 14:3: *And it shall come to pass in the day that the LORD shall give thee rest from thy sorrow, and from thy fear, and from the hard bondage wherein thou wast made to serve.*

Matthew 11:28: *Then Jesus said, "Come to me, all of you who are weary and carry heavy burdens, and I will give you rest."*

Be Your Best

I once wore a backpack of boulders.
It was burdensome on my shoulders.
My pace slowed; both legs grew weak;
So many commitments yet to keep.

The path broken, no end in sight,
The sky darkened, stealing all light.
Questions, questions and no answers found.
Each step added another dreaded pound.

The future seemed like the home of coal,
Deep, dark, dirty, in a bottomless hole.
To escape, I must rid myself of these stones;
I heft one from my pack with grunts and groans.

My arms tremble from the weight of each rock.
My mind grows numb; my body slides into shock.
With the last ounce of energy I've stored,
I crumble to my knees, "Oh, help me, Lord."

An apparition appeared, a hand larger than mine;
This manifestation is my intervention sign.
Abandon the boulder into My palm;
In a blink, you will be bathed in calm.

Words on a mere sigh, "I'll take them all."
"My child, why did you wait to call?"
As each burden falls from my hand,
Leaving in God's, one grain of sand.

A ray of sun shone through the glum.
I realized then, no matter the outcome,
Faith in Him brings tranquility and rest,
Plus all the strength needed to be my best.

This sign was mine.

Besides the calm, restful sleep and writing inspiration
that were brought to me by this study, there was one other
sign I'll share with you in a later chapter.

Chapter 6

The Signs Materialize

Only at this moment, I see what I see and feel its intense message of an all consuming love. —P. R. Fletcher

February 2013

I had lost my mom, my biggest fan and best friend, over two years ago, and now Dad, who adored me. I was an official orphan. The shiver seemed infinite since the phone call informing me that my dad had passed. He had moved on to the other side, his suffering over, leaving me here. I felt hollow, cold, and more alone than I had ever felt in my life.

The day before Dad's funeral, all the decisions had been made and the final papers signed. My husband had to run into work for a bit. I didn't want to be alone, but I couldn't bring myself to call anyone even though so many of my friends and relatives had been generous with their offers of assistance. I knew my presence would only create sadness at this time.

After a steaming, hot shower I dressed and grabbed my hooded winter coat and boots. Maybe a long walk would refresh me some. The sun was out and had melted the snow on the sidewalks on this late February afternoon. I placed my camera and phone in my coat pocket as I always do when I go for a walk.

I didn't think I had any tears left, but the faster I walked, the more they flowed. They streamed down my face beneath my sunglasses over my cheeks and dribbled down my coat onto the ground. I had no control over them. I had tissues in my pocket, but I didn't bother to use any. It felt good just to set them free. After I'd walked a long while, I stopped on a corner and raised my eyes to check my location. There in front of me, was a huge symbol, one I couldn't believe. I blinked several times, and had expected what I'd seen to have disappeared.

I blew my nose, wiped my face and stared across the street again. An instant infusion of bliss zipped through my body. An almost perfectly shaped heart had been formed of snow on a two-story rooftop. In the sun it appeared to be created of diamonds that glistened like none I've ever seen. I wanted to run up to that person's door and show them, but something held me in place. I felt this sign was singled out for me, at this moment, at this time of desperate need and immeasurable woefulness.

The tears stopped; my shoulders straightened. As I stood in the frigid weather, tranquility and love replaced the nerves that had moments before twitched through my entire body. This calm consumed me, my whole being, as if suddenly a hot out-of-the-dryer super soft blanket was draped around my body. I'm not sure how long I stood on that sidewalk in front of a stranger's home and starred, but as of that moment, there was no doubt I would make it through the funeral, and the next day, and the next, and eventually the rest of my life.

The message I received from the rooftop was to spread that special gift of warmth and love. Many loved ones would gather the following day to say their final so longs to an extraordinary man—a man I've been lucky enough to call Dad.

What did it mean? Well, to me, whenever I see a heart, even if it's on a roof and created from snow, it means Love with a capital L because at that moment I knew I was loved. I felt more love run through my body than I'd ever known, and I've had a lot of love in my life. The inner warmth, the slight tremble, and the visions that raced across my thoughts were about all the many lives that were in some way touched by my dad in his eighty-four years of life. They too were heavily grieved by his loss; it wasn't only me. I had forgotten

I was far from alone in my sorrow. They all cared and loved my dad, but they loved me as well. Message received!

This sign was mine.

I often wonder if anyone else had noticed the magical twinkle of the heart on the roof that day. Later that evening, my husband and I drove by the same house so I could show him, and, of course, the roof was dry; the heart was gone, but its message of love and warmth remains in me and always will.

CHAPTER 7

Go Away, Guilt

(It Is as It Is Meant to Be)

As you live deeper in the heart, the mirror
gets clearer and cleaner. —Rumi

The two black plastic boxes on the top shelf of my desk sat so close they appeared as one. These boxes held my parents' remains, and every time I passed them, memories flooded through my mind, some good and others not so good. At this point I felt a bit of old-fashioned catholic guilt.

Was cremation the right thing for them? Maybe they belonged buried beneath the earth in the cemetery with their parents, siblings, and friends. Had I been selfish in sharing my opinion and feelings with them?

It was because of me, their only child, that Mom and Dad had changed their plans from a traditional burial to cremation. This decision came about because of a conversation we had about cemeteries. I told them, being at one only caused me deep sadness—that grief lasted for days after the visit.

My parents enjoyed time spent at the cemetery visiting and caring for the grave sites of their loved ones. It wasn't unusual for them to take garden tools, a cooler with their lunch and beverages, and spend the entire day. This ritual brought them comfort.

Once they realized I wouldn't visit or care for their grave sites once they were gone, Mom and Dad discussed and agreed upon cremation. They wanted their ashes to be put up north at Arrow's Pond. Since the time I was a baby, we had spent many of our summer weekends at a campground called, Hillside Lagoon. At the time they seemed quite happy with their decision. This was the one place that brought more joy to their lives than any other. Dad had fished these waters with his father and brothers since he was a young boy. When Dad retired, he and Mom spent their entire summers at this same Arrow's Pond campground, one of many that encompassed the acreage of this huge pond. They loved being surrounded by the lush woods and views of the water. They fished, had campfires every night, visited with family, and made lifelong friends. Dad hunted each year when permitted.

Many of my aunts and uncles from both sides of the family leased spaces, and left their campers there year around. They also spent their vacations or weekends near us every summer. My mom's younger sister and her family became snowbirds traveling south in the winters and came north to live in their trailer at Hillside Lagoon each summer for years. It was always a blast, camping with my cousins and friends. My parents became close with the owners and were welcomed each season like family.

Things changed once the owners aged, and their health worsened. They were unable to operate the campground business any longer. When the new owners took over, most everyone left; the rules, personalities, and attitudes all changed. By the time Mom and Dad had left, there were many hurt feelings of the way some things had been handled. This caused my parents to feel unwelcome at a place they loved and had once considered their second home, a place so special that they had also decided on it being the place to spend their eternity as well. This turn of events made them uncomfortable with their decision on cremation, or at least the placement of their ashes. Death was a subject Dad wasn't too willing to discuss, so he counted on Mom to make these decisions. The subject of where to place the ashes, to my knowledge, wasn't brought up again between them after the new owners took over. They just knew they didn't feel welcome there anymore.

Since this campground was Mom and Dad's final destination plan, put into place many years ago, it seemed my decision about their remains would've been an easy one, and it would've, if there hadn't been conflict between the owner and my parents and then that conversation three years ago, unbeknownst to my dad, between Mom and me.

The Conversation

One morning I had stopped at my parents' house for a cup of coffee, as I did most days since their health had declined.

"Hi, Mom," I said in my cheerful voice from behind her. She didn't answer, but continued a steady gaze out the kitchen window. Dad was in the bathroom shaving.

I tried to follow Mom's stare, but couldn't see what she was focused on. She had grown so frail. Mom was tiny-boned, short, and averaged 120 pounds when she was healthy. She had amazing icy blue eyes framed by thick, dark brown naturally curly hair when she was young. Now it seemed, with her sparse, shortcut, all-white hair, her eyes had lost most of their luster and appeared to be more of a dull gray, matching her skin tone on this day. I remembered thinking, when did this happen? When did my parents grow old?

"Whaddya smiling about, Mom?" I asked. There was a long pause.

"The boys playing basketball over there. To have that kind of energy again. I enjoy watching them every day," she said with a long, slow sigh.

"What boys, Mom?" All I saw were the same ol' houses on the other side of the street that have always been there.

"Across the creek, over there, through the tree branches, you can see them," she said as she wagged her finger. Her voice sounded weak, tired, and a bit irritated.

Sure enough, beyond the dried foliage, across the creek, in the next city over, at least a dozen boys raced up and down a basketball court.

"They do have lots of energy," I agreed.

Barely audible, Mom said, "Put my ashes over there when I'm gone. That'll do."

My jaw dropped.

"*Mom*, really! A basketball court? You can't be serious? You don't even like basketball."

Drawing her face from the window to me, she nodded with such saddened eyes that I dropped the subject for the time-being, not knowing we'd never have the opportunity to finish this conversation. Mom passed away a few weeks later unexpectedly in 2010.

When we brought her remains home, Dad held the container to him and began to tremble. He gasped between loud sobs, "What are we going to do with her? We don't have a plan anymore."

"It'll be okay," I said as I wrapped Dad and the container he held to his heart in the tightest hug I could muster. He sobbed even harder now, shaking us both as if we were amid an earthquake.

"Dad, I have an idea," I said close to his ear, so he could hear. "Your happiest times and memories were made at Arrow's Pond over many years, not just the last conflicted couple, right?" He gave a slight nod. I grabbed the tissues and wiped my own tears. I handed Dad a few.

My mind swirled as I tried to come up with something, anything; and then the words spewed from my mouth, "Why don't we keep Mom here at the house with you until you're called home, in another hundred years or so?" I couldn't bear to think of him being gone too. "When your remains arrive, I'll mix your ashes with Mom's and take you both to your favorite fishing waters, but I'll launch from one of the other campgrounds that surrounds the same magical pond that you've both loved, laughed, fished, and enjoyed most all of your lives at."

The quakes lessened; Dad's head lifted, and his eyes brightened. A slow smile came to his face. I knew he loved the idea. But what bothered me most was that he didn't know of the conversation I had had with Mom about the stupid basketball court. Would Mom love this idea as well? Oh, how I wanted to ask her and have her permission. She just couldn't have been serious. I think I knew this in my heart, but it still felt as if I was disobeying her final wishes. *If she could only tell me; if only I could have another sign.*

I touched the containers that held their remains every morning and every evening. A mere whisper from within reminded me it was almost time. I knew they didn't belong on my desk in those ugly black boxes, or any kind of a box. It was time to face the irreversible decision of what to do with their remains I had made two days after Dad passed away, and almost three years after Mom. I felt almost a hundred percent positive it was the right choice after I received another message from the Bible study.

Dad had passed before I finished the Bible study, and I had promised the author I would complete it soon on my own, no matter what. I only had five days of the study left to do.

Since Dad had wanted everything the same as Mom for his funeral, there wasn't much for me to do or plan. They each wanted one day visitation with no church or procession. I had two days before the funeral; I thought it would be a good time to finish the last five lessons in the Bible study; I was so close to the end. As I searched for a particular verse that was requested in the study guide, I came across a psalm not related to the lesson and not even close to the page I was supposed to be on. I swear it practically jumped off the page. My eyes were drawn to the words that took my breath away and left me without a doubt what I was meant to do with my parents' ashes.

I read Psalm 29:10: The Lord rules over the floodwaters (not basketball courts; ah ha, I knew it!).

Again when I needed it most, there it was in black and white and written over two thousand years ago. In my world and in anybody's world that has ever camped or fished at the same campground we did, the word *floodwaters* is one of the most used terms of reference when speaking of Arrow's Pond. It used to be acres of forests and cedar swamp until, in the 1930s, it was flooded and stocked with a variety of fish.

Again I sobbed in gratefulness and relief for my prayer being answered. I felt confident in my decision, but still fretted over how to go about actually doing the deed of dispersing their ashes—something that never seems to come up in conversation.

What I didn't realize was that my parents' final destination would be an experience I never could've planned or even imagined.

This decision could not be changed once done. But in my heart I knew it felt right. And the signs didn't stop here. There's more … much more.

This sign was mine!

CHAPTER 8

The Love Doves

This Universe is filled with natural wonders. Shall we open our eyes and ears, turn off our skeptic minds and let miracles touch our soul. —P. R. Fletcher

2013:

It was March; not even a month since Dad had passed away. I wondered everyday about death and all that happens after a loved one dies. I knew what I had been taught and believed all these years; only now, I had questions—questions that raged within, and there was an emptiness, and lack of belief that I couldn't understand or explain.

I wondered if my parents found each other for all Eternity. After almost sixty years of marriage here on earth, had it been Mom who greeted Dad on his deathbed? The death or near-death experiences I've read about seem to vary from person to person, book to book.

I often spoke to the containers on my desk, asking that very question. I thought I would know, sense it somehow, when that magical, divine reconnection happened in the spiritual world. I had no idea how long it would take. At that moment all I had was doubt, yet something niggled away at me, saying I needed to trust. I had to listen to that tiny whisper of intuition from within. I had been given signs before, and now on this morning, I asked to be given another.

Good Morning America blared on the television as I warmed my hands around a mug of coffee. Mom and Dad stared at me from a framed photograph. It had been taken professionally in the early eighties. I smiled every day at that picture and had for many years. Only now, since they were both passed on, it was through blurred, tear-filled eyes.

Mom in her mauve sweater and pearls and Dad in his flannel shirt, although he dressed it up with a turtleneck beneath after mild prompting and *the look* from Mom. I smiled at the memory. I missed them so much it was hard to breathe sometimes.

My thoughts were distracted by a deep garbled coo of a dove, louder than the TV, and could be heard even with the windows secured on this chilly morning. Being a bird lover, as my parents had been, whenever I hear that sound I have to find the bird that is calling and see if I can find its mate nearby. Mom especially liked doves and never missed the opportunity to tell me that mourning doves mate for life, just like us. I remembered how we about peed ourselves laughing so hard when we discovered their life span is only about a year and a half; heck, anyone could do that.

On this day, I didn't have to search far. The mourning doves were less than six feet away. The male was crouched on the railing of the deck and stared in at me through the sliding door wall window. Next to him was his mate, nestled to his side.

As I watched them I thought of how comfortable they appeared together. They seemed so relaxed and at peace, even with me only a few steps away. The doves preened themselves and then each other. One would move casually along the rail, and the other would scoot closer. They nuzzled their necks and nibbled at one another. I couldn't help but grin as I thought, *Maybe you guys should get a room.*

As I observed the doves a while longer, a strong desire came over me to preserve this moment. I hesitated, not wanting to leave them and how they made me feel, then tiptoed into the other room to get my camera. I figured they would be gone by the time I returned, but, to my surprise, they were still there. I snapped several pictures and even slid the patio door open just enough to get the camera outside to get a better shot. They didn't budge. Their tiny heads tilted, looking at me looking at them. I had never been so close to a mourning dove before.

Not wanting to leave the entertainment of the birds, I knew I had things to do. It was while I unloaded the dishwasher that it hit me. I knew. It was the first time in weeks I didn't have that tenseness in my neck and shoulders. Those usual doubts and questions weren't racing through my brain. I felt the doves' peace, their love, their joy, their togetherness. Message received!

Mom and Dad were together again. The calm that radiated from those two birds on my deck was not to be denied. A quick quiver traveled over my skin and left in its wake complete comfort. I soft stepped to the doorwall, my heart filled with love, and as I did, the doves took flight side by side as if they knew their job was done, their message delivered. They were on my deck for three hours that day— my answer received that cold morning in early March within a month of Dad's death.

The dove carries symbolic meaning not only in the Christian community but in many other cultures throughout the world. With Noah, it was a dove that brought the olive branch back to the ark, bringing with it hope. In Mathew 3:16 it's said, "Spirit of God descended like a dove upon us." This verse radiates peace. For me, I'm going with, they are a symbol of divine infinite love and together for all of their lives, no matter how long the life span.

Those angels I've heard about all my life aren't always invisible, especially if we open our minds and our hearts and let their peace rest upon our souls.

The doves have never visited my deck and stayed that long before, and I suspect they will never again, unless they have another message to deliver.

This sign was mine.

CHAPTER 9

What Remains

You gain strength, courage, and confidence by every experience in which you really stop to look fear in the face. You must do the thing which you think you cannot do. —Eleanor Roosevelt

Taking the final step with my parents' ashes was something I knew I'd have to take care of eventually. I didn't know if there was any kind of etiquette to the time frame or even legalities. Should you keep the ashes for a year, five years, bury them, and can you or should you divide them or keep them complete? What I knew for sure was this finality, one of no changing your mind was about to happen, and it placed a fear in me that ran like the deepest river through my body. I didn't know, when it came right down to it, if I was even capable of dispersing their ashes, the final separation, the only part of their human form and existence left here on earth.

What I had learned from my parents and throughout my life from attending many funerals was that a loved one's dying wishes should be respected, no matter how normal or strange their wishes may seem to others.

So far my plan was to take a few days later in the month and go to Arrow's Pond, a mile up the road from the campground where we used to lease a lot and stay, still the same waters, but a different camping area, this other camp is called Wolf's Landing. Dad and I had rented a cabin there the summer after Mom passed. He and I enjoyed our three-day visit and spoke of the tremendous ache we both felt from no longer having our own trailers and familiar campground to run away to. I missed being in nature and felt empty these last few years without it. I explained this to Dad, and he understood and agreed he felt the same.

As we sat on the small deck and watched the few fishing boats out on the water, I asked, "Dad, do you remember the painting I bought at that garage sale down the street from your house last year?"

He grinned, nodded, and said, "How could I forget? I thought you were going to keel over when you came in the door so excited and out of breath."

I'd run back to his house, my treasure wrapped in my arms—a framed painting with a perfect title of *Simple Pleasures*. I'd told him that I found my new summer place in that painting. I knew in my heart—,somehow, some way—that it would be mine someday. It was an undeniable déjà vu moment, so much so that it caused me to tremble.

The painting was of a small, older wood cabin on a hill with a nearby wooded area. A beat-up weathered dock and rowboat sat on the water below. "That's all I want, Dad. That's all I need." I wanted my granddaughter to grow up to enjoy and appreciate nature as I had, as my parents had taught me and their grandsons.

Dad told many of his nurses and doctors about that painting from the garage sale and how I was searching for that shack on a lake. Chuckling, he'd end with, "I have no doubt she'll find it, too."

Dad and I had reminisced for days about all the funny fish tales we'd heard over the years, battling the snakes in the outhouses, and the one lone bear visit that scared the bejeebers out of us. We found ourselves teary-eyed as we spoke of the many relatives and friends that had camped with us and their silly incidences over the years, and now many had passed on. We had grand, wonderful memories. Dad, even though weak and depressed at the time of this trip, radiated such a sense of peace when he looked out at his beloved floodwaters.

I didn't know it at the time, but it was this visit to Wolf's Campground with Dad that was the reason I had come up with the suggestion about it being the new perfect place for the dispersal of their ashes.

In June of 2013, my aunt Corrine came in from out of town. She had not been back to her hometown in six years due to her husband's health decline. She missed staying the summers at Hillside Lagoon next door to Mom and Dad, and the *roughing it* days, as much as we did, but more so, she missed my mom, her oldest sister, and even worse she had missed Mom's funeral and was devastated. She was unable to attend Dad's funeral as well for the same reason.

The day after she arrived, we had gotten together for breakfast and chatted nonstop as we tried to catch up on the past six years. She asked about my parents' funerals and apologized once again for not being there. She then asked about their ashes and if I had planned to keep them at the house.

I told her my thought so far was to take a quick trip up north to the floodwaters the following week and explained I would be staying at Wolf's Campground or landing as it's sometimes called. She struggled with her emotion as she asked, "Would you mind if I come along since I couldn't attend either of their funerals?"

I was honored and surprised at her offer and without hesitation said, "Well, of course. I'm sure Mom and Dad would be thrilled to have you there, as would I. They mentioned you often, and both missed you and Uncle Larry terribly."

I could hardly believe someone would offer to do this sad, sad thing, and the other strong emotion for me was that of pure relief. I felt a strong sense that she was the perfect person to go with me.

I said, "I don't know if there is a right way or a wrong way to do this, but I'm going to do my best to honor Mom and Dad in some way." She agreed that whatever way I did, would be right. She had never done anything like this before either. I had the start of a plan.

When I shared my excitement with Ella, one of my lifelong best girlfriends, about my aunt going with me and how I felt this was meant to be, her eyes flooded in an instant, and tears spilled over, surprising me. She too loved my mom and dad. She and I had met in high school and have remained close throughout the years. She camped every summer with my family and later with her own family. She also was unable to attend either of my parents' funerals due to being out of the state on both funeral dates. She often mentioned how sick to her stomach awful she felt every time she thought about not being there. Her voice trembled, "Would it be okay if I came along with you and your aunt since I didn't make the funerals either? It would mean a lot to me."

We hugged and cried. I said, "Of course, and thank you. Aunt Corrine will be thrilled to see you again too." They had met many times while camping at Arrow's Pond.

I didn't have to do this very special final good-bye alone. I had two people I loved more than I can describe going with me. I could've never asked anyone to go with me and wouldn't have, not even my husband. I had planned on doing this alone. We chose the next Monday to take my parent's ashes and spend a night or two at Wolf's.

The Signs Begin

First sign. The only available room for the days we wanted was the exact same cabin Dad and I stayed in two summers ago after Mom had passed on. It felt so right, I couldn't have planned it any better.

Second sign. I rented a boat and motor and made the decision we'd go out the next afternoon after we arrived. I wanted to put the ashes in the water across from our old campground, the one where lifetimes of extraordinary family camping memories were made. This was probably a mile or two out. (These waters cover well over thirteen square miles of land.)

The next afternoon, we hauled several tote bags down to the shoreline, not a fishing pole in sight. The owner gave us an odd look, but showed us which boat to use and went over the motor instructions with me, then shoved us off. I somehow always managed to flood Dad's old nine-horse Johnson. Well, no excuse on this newer one. I pulled the cord, and it started. I nodded! I pushed in the choke, and it promptly stalled. I tried again and again. Voilà—flooded! I couldn't help but laugh at myself. The owner, who stood on the shore, watched us with a grin. He jumped in another boat and came to our rescue several yards out.

He reached over from his boat and yanked on our motor's cord … first pull, of course, just like Dad, it started with a puff of smoke and strong gas fumes. I flushed with embarrassment like the old days. He suggested we stay close so we could yell if we needed anything. He didn't know these three determined ladies in this boat very well. We all nodded and took off in the opposite direction with the motor going full out. Some things never change. I didn't give the motor another thought. Dad's had never stalled again once I got her going the first time.

Once I saw the shoreline of Hillside Lagoon in the distance, I killed the motor, and Ella dropped the anchor in what I knew to be one of Mom and Dad's favorite fishing spots. I knew this by the location of the Osprey's nest and a large fallen tree that we often referred to as the, picnic table, a place you never wanted your boat to get stuck on. The sun's rays on my back didn't help the quivers that spiraled through my body. No other boats were around us. It was a gorgeous day.

"This is it," I said in a shaky voice, "Looks like the perfect spot to me." *How many times had I heard my dad say those exact words? He'd cut the motor, and I would drop the anchor or tie our rope to an old tree trunk as we grabbed our poles.*

Corrine and Ella both nodded.

Third sign. While the song "My Way" played loudly on a portable CD player, sung by Mom and Dad's favorite, Elvis Presley, I found myself lost in memories of my childhood. So much music and dancing, all the fishing, gardening, canning vegetables, Mom's practical jokes, and my parents' faces when they saw each of their grandsons for the first time, and later their adored great-granddaughter—they, my parents, were the real deal; they were love. There were so many good times—so much laughter—and they were both so loved by so many.

When the song ended, I took a deep breath and told the story about how my parents had bought me this Elvis eight-track tape for Christmas when I was a teenager. They wanted to listen to it (to make sure it worked, yeah, right!) and had ended up dancing all night and wearing it out by the time Christmas Eve arrived. They had to buy me another before Christmas morning. I later replaced it and gave them this CD. And it remained their favorite and never left their car, until now.

After the song, I read several Bible verses. We lifted our water bottles filled with wine and toasted to the wonderful times in the past and to the time when we shall all meet again. With a slow hand that trembled, I began to sprinkle

Mom and Dad's mixed remains into the waters as promised. My slow tears mixed with their ashes as they slid over the side of the boat. I've never liked good-byes, and this was the hardest one of my life.

I'm not sure why or where it came from, but a sudden panic shook me. Heavy doubt slithered into my mind. The sobs escaped. Was it the right thing to do? Is this really what they both wanted? The guilt returned, squeezing the breath from me, while the ashes slid bit by bit into the water.

The last of the ashes were almost gone. It's so final! How can I live with myself if this was the wrong thing to do? As these thoughts flashed through my mind, I sobbed louder, and my shoulders shook. I had done so well up to this point. Now, I wanted to jump in the water and be with them.

The warmth of two sets of loving arms moved in and wrapped around my heaving shoulders, comforting me and holding me together. How could I have done this alone? To answer that question, I couldn't have, and I wasn't meant to.

The sobs ceased, and my body relaxed. We were all still seated close together, still in a hug when I turned my eyes back to the water and released the final trickles of Mom and Dad's remains. I watched as the ashes seemed to form a bright arch in the water. Within moments there were individual streams; visible golden rays glistened and swirled, distinct spears of white light shot beneath the surface, sinking and spreading through the water away from the boat. These thread-like gold ragged lines shimmered and shined. It was like an underwater firework display. I noticed all of this as I squinted into the water in disbelief. I lifted my sunglasses and let them fall back into place. I whispered, not knowing if I was seeing things, "Can you guys see that?"

Both my aunt and friend were staring at the water and could only nod, their eyes pooled with tears. This time they were tears of joy.

"I believe they're home." I asked, "Can you feel their peace?" They both nodded.

Once again, there was an all consuming peace that settled upon me. It was that everything is going to be okay kind of peace—that feeling of pure joy and love, like sometimes when an infant or young child or spouse touches you in a certain way, and you feel this amazing sensation sprint throughout your body. (I call these sensations inside-out goose bumps.) It's a special kind of peace, certainty, and love like no other.

This time for me, it began as a surface tingle, a slight wave at the top center of my head, and then went deeper. It proceeded to feather touch every organ and nerve in my body until it made its way to the tips of my toes. I felt its travels within, and there was a complete internal knowing of awareness, and love that was left in its trail.

My heartfelt explanation for this phenomenon is that my unconditional love touched the unconditional love of both my parents at that moment, and also of my aunt and friend. It moved and flowed, and somehow intertwined with me, them, and my mind, body, and soul.

This moment in time has been the most powerful of my life so far.

All of us felt something unique and extraordinary, and the words that came up several times in our discussion afterward were deep connection and spiritual experience. We agreed that everything happened just the way it was meant to, at the exact moment it was needed with the people it was meant to be shared with.

This experience shared with Mom and Dad will be with each of us always, no matter where we are on this earth or in Eternity. I am forever grateful!

This sign was mine.

Chapter 10

Too Good to Be True, or Is It?

What you seek is seeking you. —Rumi

Thinking about a property search filled me with excitement and some threads of doubt. There's never a perfect time, like having enough of everything before having a baby. I knew it may take me a long while to find the place I'd envisioned, the place I knew in my heart was somewhere out there for me, *maybe a place like in my yard sale painting that I look at daily and envision it being mine someday.*

That tiny voice whispered from within, and the message was clear—search and you shall find. Or was that my mother voice? Was this a nudge coming from my parents? I knew I had to begin my search; now was the time. I hadn't thought it would begin so soon and had no intention of it beginning when we took my parents' ashes to the pond.

When we had gone to town for gas, I pulled into the parking lot of the real estate office first. I hadn't planned on this stop, but since I was there, I might as well go in, right? Maybe I would get lucky, and the property I searched for would be somewhere around those eight thousand acres of water that we loved so much. Maybe I wouldn't have to leave this place after all. That would be something.

My hope was that I'd been drawn there for a reason; maybe it was another sign, but as it turned out, the property surrounding Arrow's Pond was mostly state-owned land dotted with several camping and hunting businesses. Very little was for sale at that time. According to the real estate woman at the office, nothing that I had described in my price range would be up for sale anytime soon in the area. *This wasn't meant to be. It was time to move on from Arrow's Pond.*

So my next thought was if I can't have the summer place I grew up on, then I will try to find something closer to home. Dad had mentioned many times how he had wished their getaway wasn't such a long drive. I decided I'd look for places no more than three hours from where I live. That would be much better than the over five-hour drive in the car for each trip to Arrow's Pond, and less expensive for gas too.

My friend Ella suggested we could check for properties on our return trip. She checked her phone for real estate offices along our route toward home. She found an agent with some free time to show us a few lake-view properties in the area a bit over three hours from where we live. I was thrilled with that idea.

This was my first reality check on waterfront property, and what I could get within my budget. This confirmed it—a shack on a lake, that would be about it, and I would be fine with that. I needed to be outdoors in nature, somewhere and it had to be soon.

Out of the seven properties the Realtor showed me that day, there was one that I would consider, and it hadn't been listed yet. It was a two-bedroom 1960s mobile home well taken care of and not much property. It was on a small private lake that looked to me like an oversized backyard pond compared to Arrow's. The Realtor called me two days later and said the seller sold it to family instead of listing. I guess that wasn't meant to be either.

I used the process-of-elimination after those initial visits and at least discovered what I didn't want and what I needed to look for inside and out.

Ella also suggested I search online for waterfronts for sale by owner.

I hadn't thought about that and was a bit apprehensive because I know nothing about real estate, having only moved once in my life over thirty-five years ago.

One evening after my return from the ashes trip, my husband went to bed, and I searched Craigslist for writing gigs, which I did often. This particular night my eyes landed upon a different category, one I hadn't noticed before— Waterfront Property; of course, I clicked on it. The first hit led me to an ad that made me think, *Yeah, right, this is way too good to be true.* The property was less than two hours away. They referred to it as a mobile cottage, and it came fully furnished with lake access and a perfect view, along with some wooded areas. It included a dock, tiny pontoon, and a paddleboat. All of this was within the price range that I could afford. I thought, no way, the area must be bad; there's mold for sure. Going from what properties I had already viewed, this place seemed impossible or a miracle online.

A vision of Mom passed through my mind, head cocked, twinkle in her eye, and wide smile; her finger wagged, aimed at me, and I could almost hear her words, "If it sounds too good to be true, well, it probably is." Then came Dad's slow smile, a wink and his quiet words, "but then it never hurts to check it out."

I went to bed with the images from the Internet and of my parents in the forefront of my mind. In the morning I pulled up the ad again, which led to the call. There had to be a catch, and I needed to find out what it was.

The owner's daughter's sweet voice introduced herself as Kara, and answered all my questions. She said, "The pictures and the prices were accurate. It's better in person than online—a must-see."

"What's the catch?" I asked.

"No catch," she said. "You can keep to yourself, or you can golf nine holes in the attached course. There is always something fun going on within the resort, if you choose."

"Do you mind me asking, if it's so great, why are you selling?"

There was a long hesitation and then she said, "My mom's health has declined, and she's too ill to maintain this, her summer home, anymore."

I understood those words only too well. She wanted to know when would be a good time for me to see the place. I said I had to think about it and would give her a call back.

I didn't want to be in a resort; I wanted a place to call my own. So I scratched it off my list. But something about those images wouldn't go away.

Later the next evening I mentioned the too good to be true property to my husband.

He wanted me to find a place that I adored, since I was the one with the vision and would be making more visits to it than he would since he wasn't retired yet. I longed for a serene space to connect with nature. I wanted a place to hike and fish, and to get-away from it all. I wanted my granddaughter to experience these things also. I had also hoped to create an inspirational writing space and host small retreats along with family get-togethers.

It bothered me that this property was so close. How could it feel like that up north camp feel, being under two hours away from home? And then the fact that it was in a resort/RV campground and only open six months of the year.

I was shocked when my husband stated that he loved the distance and the resort idea. He asked why I didn't. When I responded, he made valid points about my not liking to drive in the winter. He was right; I wouldn't drive even if there was a threat of snow on the roads. But his favorite thing was that the property would be maintained by someone besides himself. (He had taken care of several properties for a long time and didn't need any more.) I never showed him the pictures of the place. But I made the decision to make an appointment and check out what I referred to as the shack on a lake, even though it appeared to be much more than that.

I had searched and viewed a dozen or more cabins and properties by now and knew better than to get my hopes up. What they showed online wasn't always accurate. The pungent musty odors and rotting wood were never included in the Realtors' ads, and neither were the conditions of the neighboring properties or their owners.

After checking the calendar, I decided to make the property visit appointment (if it was available) on the same day I'd planned on driving an hour north to stay overnight with my writing friend, Maggie. We'd both been invited to a brunch that was closer to her home than mine. She had invited me to come the day before the brunch and have dinner. We could enjoy a writing chat, and I could spend the night and then head to her friend's house in the morning for brunch. It was the perfect plan, and even if I didn't like the property, I wouldn't be wasting time or gas because I had other fun things planned.

I searched online to see if there were any other for-sale properties in the surrounding area that I could at least drive by, since I had the whole afternoon before the resort appointment and meeting my friend Maggie.

I found one. It was a vacant cottage seated on a fast-moving river, just ten minutes away from the resort property, and was within my price range. Worth a drive by, I thought.

I called another special lifelong high school friend, Faith, and asked if she wanted to meet for lunch, since I was going to be in a neighboring city to view some properties not too far from where she lived.

It worked out perfect because she and her daughter Daizi, were free to play all day and thought it would be exciting to accompany me to both sites. I was grateful to have them along, and it was an extra bonus that they were familiar with the area.

The drive-by property was a one-bedroom fixer upper cottage with lovely views. The river's dam was about ten steps from the back door and gorgeous. The dam's flow was so intense you had to raise your voice so the person next to you could hear what you were saying. But the main problem was, you couldn't fish in that area, and fishing was a definite high priority for me.

I groaned, "Too noisy and no fishing; a fabulous view, though." As we got back into the car, and I turned the key, a weird shiver spiraled through my body. I set the GPS for the address to the too-good-to-be-true destination. Within a short distance from the river cottage, the voice from the GPS had us turn onto Old Louis Road. Faith and I both looked at each other, our wide eyes filled. She said what I was thinking. In a barely audible whisper, Faith's lips formed the words, "Dad is leading us to this place." Louis is my father's name. Faith has referred to my mom and dad as just that, since she lived with us for several years back in our high school days and has continued to be as close to us as any family member.

A tall white fence along the highway with a welcome sign greeted us as we turned into the, The R&R Resort. I thought, *Oh no, this isn't at all what I want.* Even though well groomed, it was packed with campers and mobiles, and golf carts that zipped everywhere. When we arrived at the correct lot number, down a narrow black-topped street, a dead-end, we were greeted by the owner's two daughters, Kim and Kara, and her husband, Dan, as we got out of the car. My legs quivered and felt unsteady, and my stomach tightened. Maybe my lunch didn't agree with me.

This tiny plot of land and the cottage sat on a grassy hill. I looked out over the water to a wooded area across the lake. My emotion shook beneath the surface of my skin and was ready to burst forth. In all honesty, I knew in that split second, even before going inside, that this was it; this was my shack on the lake, even though it was far from being a shack.

The view was amazing and better than I had ever imagined, even in my dreams! Kara had been right about it being a must-see. For me it was a *must feel*, and Lord did I feel.

We did a quick walk through the one-bedroom cottage and ended on the front deck, which overlooked the water. Several people strolled by on a blacktopped, narrow, winding walking path that hugged the bottom of the hill in between the water and the cottage. I shook my head. *Oh, how many problems I'd solved by taking long walks around my crowded city neighborhood.* The scenery here was much different and so gorgeous, and now my throat felt as tight as my stomach.

Every direction I turned while on the deck brought on a gasp! It was one of those rare moments that rendered me speechless. I adored the hill that the mobile cottage sat on, the lone tree and red-bricked fire pit to its side, and even the matching shed was perfect. Below us there was a slight ripple on the water. I felt my eyes fill and battled to keep this crazy emotion under control. One main thing I know about real estate is you're not supposed to show excitement to the sellers. Probably wouldn't be a good thing to throw up on them either.

Mom and Dad would adore this place. Their excited faces wouldn't leave my mind. I wished they were here with me, in person. It was, no doubt, love at first sight. The more we talked, the more comfortable I grew with these people, and, even more importantly, I felt a sense of ... a sense of something. It felt familiar, almost like home. It was, without a doubt, another powerful déjà vu moment.

I could tell Kara and Kim were emotional about selling. We talked for over an hour about caring for incapacitated parents. Their widowed mother now stayed with Kara and Dan a few miles away.

I understood only too well and shared a bit about my last two years with Dad. We all hugged with an effort to control our tears.

We walked through the cottage once more, and I noticed a few details that went unnoticed my first time through.

Small things like the handles on the cupboards were the exact same ones I had chosen for our previous cabinets at home. The kitchen floor was so close to the same design and colorations as the one we have now. I loved the tiny bathroom—first, the fact that it was a plumbed, functional bathroom with a real shower and toilet that flushes. The next best part was the wallpaper design. The wide border was trimmed in forest green and lined with wooden outhouses, each one having a short whimsical saying above it. Outhouses and Arrow's Pond have been all I've ever known while camping. How ironic that this place had a real bathroom decorated in outhouses; it caused me to chuckle.

The owner's daughters and I talked about their family gatherings. This was their mom's summer home, and she adored living in it for six months each year. She lived the other six months in a warmer climate. My own visions danced as the owner's daughters reminisced and described their visits with their mom, telling me of all the card games, bonfires, shooting stars, delicious foods, and beverages shared with family and friends over the years at this cottage.

Kara swiped at her eyes where dark shadows rested, and she said, "My kids and the other grandkids had tons of fun here. They liked fishing and the beach. There's bass and assorted pan fish. It's so quiet and peaceful. Only electric motors are allowed on the lake."

I asked with curiosity, "Have you had many people looking?"

"A few," Dan answered. "Another interested party is coming by to view the place this evening."

At that moment, my body tensed, and I thought I was going to hyperventilate. This wasn't at all brought on by the sellers; there was no pressure from them. This feeling came from something deep within my gut, and I had to stop the tremble in my voice. I cleared my throat and asked, "What would it take for you to cancel that last showing?"

Kim and Kara's eyes widened. "Are you serious?" they asked at the same time.

"Very."

She glanced at her sister, who said, "We'll need a $500 deposit."

I slid my checkbook from my purse, and noticed her head shake. "I'm sorry. We can't accept a check," Kim said. "Two weeks ago when we first advertised, a couple came in, looked everything over, and claimed they adored every inch of the place, and went on and on. The man wrote a check right there and then for the whole asking amount, and sadly the check bounced. This has caused us much unneeded grief at this time. We, me and my other siblings, have agreed that we would accept cash only for the deposit." Her head drooped, and she appeared exhausted.

I frowned; my heart did a free fall to my feet. My mind raced as I tried to think of the balance in our checking account and wondered if I could find an automatic teller machine somewhere. I bet Faith knew where one was. It was at that moment that another memory flashed through my mind.

"You aren't going to believe this," I said as I dug through my purse once more. "I happen to have a lot of cash on me, which I never carry. I don't think it's enough, though."

* * *

Okay, well, here's another one of those crazy, coincidental things. That morning before I left the house, I did a double-check to make sure I had my camera, GPS, checkbook, and overnight items for staying at Maggie's house. I was almost out the door, and something made me turn back to my room and grab the zipper bag I had stuffed with cash from the past weekend's garage sale. I had earned the most ever by clearing out items from Mom and Dad's house as we prepared it to put on the market. I had priced everything low as a tribute to Mom and her love of a bargain. I had planned on using this money for our annual ladies' three day retreat at one of the largest flea markets in the nation, Shipshewana IN. My intention being to purchase a special memorial dedicated to Mom and Dad, possibly a large cement piece for the yard.

As tacky as it appeared, I whipped out my baggie of cash and counted out $475. Faith and Daizi were out on the deck enjoying the view, leaving me to chat with the sellers, but must have caught the bit where I groaned and said I was short. She rushed to my side and generously offered me cash from her wallet to make up the needed difference for the deposit.

At this point the owner's daughter nodded with a grand smile and said, "We'll take $400 and make the call to cancel the other showing. You may need some cash for tomorrow's brunch you mentioned earlier." We hugged tightly. I felt such a strong connection with these ladies. Heck, we were complete strangers less than two hours ago, and now I felt as if we were almost family, and this place already had such a feeling of home.

We ended the visit with a conversation about how their mother wanted the right person to purchase her summer home, not just anyone. The girls said they knew their mom would love that I'm a book lover and a writer as well, since she was an avid reader. They said that finding the right owner was important to all of them. They added that the couple that had bounced the check wasn't meant to have this wonderful place. They hadn't gotten the best vibes from the woman. They now felt the bounced check was meant to happen because this was a perfect fit for me and my family.

Everything happens for a reason, and I knew they were right.

We agreed I would come back to sign the papers the following weekend. As I was leaving with my heart over filled at finding this place, Kara and Kim introduced me to my new next door neighbor. This complete stranger wrapped me in a warm hug and held tight, chuckled, and said, "Just call me Glow Baby. I'll tell you the story later." I knew in my heart that anyone with such a great deep rooted hefty laugh and stories to tell was a kindred spirit for sure, and we'd get along just fine. They all waved their goodbyes as I pulled away and let the happy tears flow as I couldn't contain them any longer.

There's More!

As it turned out, maybe this was a coincidence, or maybe not? I had written the date for the brunch and the night I planned to spend at Maggie's in two places, the kitchen calendar and my office. Both places it was written the same. Yet, I went on the wrong day. Imagine my surprise and Maggie's when I texted her after the showing to say I was on my way. She responded by saying our dinner date wasn't until the next day, and the brunch was Saturday morning, not Friday.

I felt so stupid on my way home until I realized I was in the exact right place at the right time. (The brunch Maggie and I were to attend was at the home of the Bible study's author. These two friends played an important part in the synchronicity of these events and in my life.)

I feel in my heart that I would've missed out on this lovely place if I hadn't viewed that property that day at that time, before the other prospective buyer.

The following weekend the papers were signed. I couldn't believe I now owned a place to find my inner peace, write, and make tons of memories with my family and friends along the way—a place for more of my dreams to come true!

And There's More!

The day after I became the owner of this lovely summer cottage, I received a despondent text from Kara. It announced that her mother had passed away peacefully in her sleep during the night. One of their last conversations had been about how they all knew that the right family had found and bought her mother's much-loved summer home. Coincidence?

It was awhile before I realized the significant similarities between our new place and the painting I had purchased at that garage sale two years prior. It was another convincing déjà vu moment.

It's not too good to be true, if you have loved ones in high places … (*Wink,*) Forever grateful, Mom and Dad.

CHAPTER 11

Coming Full Circle

What you leave behind is not what is engraved in stone monuments, but what is woven into the lives of others. —Pericles

June 2014:

While going through my parents' things after Dad died, I discovered his size twelve gold wedding band in a box. It hadn't been worn in years due to his job in a factory making it unsafe for him to wear while he worked. Later he had lost so much weight it wouldn't stay on his finger. None of that changed the reality that he and Mom were happily married almost sixty years when she passed.

Dad had given me all Moms' jewelry after her funeral—some only thin gold bands, and most of the other pieces were missing stones.

I had tried each one on and then lovingly tucked them away in a special ceramic box. I sadly added Dad's ring to the container. I'd been overwhelmed with an urge to do something special with their jewelry. But, I didn't know what. I couldn't allow these sacred rings to sit in the dark in the bottom of a dresser drawer.

What do most people do with their parents' jewelry once they're gone? I had no idea, so I began asking. The most common answer given was that it was split up among the children and grandchildren. More often than not, the jewelry was stored in a safe place and never worn by family.

Someone mentioned to me about places that create jewelry from your loved one's remains. They can create stones from the ashes. I had no idea about any of this. Other retailers sell tiny clear tubes that can be attached to a chain or put into a ring setting with your loved ones ashes protected within. I had never heard of this type of jewelry. Being curious, I checked online. Sure enough, there were many to choose from. Having to consciously relax my facial muscles was a certain sign that this route wasn't the one for me.

One local jeweler suggested Dad's large band could be re-formed into a lovely twisted heart and worn as a pendant. Hearts being my favorite shape of all time, I had to give the idea some serious consideration. If I did this, I would still have to come up with something to do with Mom's gold and diamonds. Nope, I knew I wanted their rings together, as they have always been. My search continued. I had to keep the faith that something would come, and I would recognize it when it did.

Another jeweler I spoke with, one that came with an outstanding recommendation, said he could take the gold from both my parents' rings and create a whole new piece. The more we spoke, the more I loved his ideas.

I'd seen samples of his work over the years, worn by my sister-in-law at Christmastime. This jeweler does phenomenal exclusive design work. I was excited.

While I sat with my in-laws' trusted jeweler, I was barely able to speak, and my one foot bounced out of control. I chewed on the corner of my lip until I tasted blood. I reverently caressed the ring box that sat in the center of my lap as the first tear slid from my eye. Was I really going to leave my parents' sacred wedding rings with this complete stranger, who was going to destroy them and then reconstruct them? *Was I crazy? Why was I doing this? How could it be the right thing? What if they get stolen or something else goes wrong? I can never get them back.*

The jeweler doodled on a piece of paper while I worked on my composure. He handed me a tissue and spoke about pendant styles and things he could do with the gold and the stones. It wasn't a pendant I wanted or needed. It was … one last ring to make my set of ten complete.

"Can you make a thumb ring?" I asked.

"No problem," he answered with a strong nod as he continued drawing. He asked to see my hands. I untangled them from my lap, leaving the box containing my parents' gold in place. Carefully he studied the nine rings on my trembling hands, especially my other thumb ring. His eyes brightened as he said, "I have an idea of what we can do."

Within minutes, he showed me his sketch, and then he spoke the words that fit so much into my life. I was convinced at this point my choice about everything here at this moment was again right and was meant to be.

The jeweler said, "You need bookends to bring everything together." He had no idea I was a writer or a lifelong lover of books. His words were pure comfort to me, and his design was even better.

The sketch mimicked the style of my other thumb ring, created in a way that when slipped over the large knuckle, it could be squeezed slightly to prevent spinning. Only this ring will be exclusive. One hundred percent exclusive— created from the gold and diamonds of over a half century ago and worn by two people that fell in love, married, and were convinced they couldn't have children, until nine years later when I was conceived!

They are the entire reason I'm here today and am the person I am meant to be. This decision couldn't be more right, and I knew that as of that moment.

Relieved and filled with joy, I relinquished the box of Mom and Dad's gold and asked him to make it into the ring I had searched for in the past and would treasure for the rest of my life.

He created the final design from Mom's three engagement diamonds, her empty band, and the gold chain along with the earring casings and Dad's wedding ring. The jeweler said it needed some other stones for balance and color to accent Mom's diamonds. I agreed.

He mentioned a few available stones that he thought would make a nice contrast. I tried to envision gemstones, such as rubies or sapphires, emeralds or opals. There are so many, I became overwhelmed.

"Or there's always diamonds," The jeweler suggested. "They come in enhanced colors now; we could go with more diamonds, if you'd like."

He had my attention. Purple was the second color he named.

"Stop right there," I said. "It can't get any better than that. Mom's diamonds, Dad's gold, and purple diamond accents! Perfect!"

It's a ring I wear everyday like the others, but this one has the most meaning to me. When the sun glints off the facets of this ring, I know my parents are with me. I am forever reminded of how much I am loved, and why I was created, and that I'm here in this world for a purpose and that I have made a difference.

Once again there had been a reason I hadn't found a thumb ring in all the past years I've searched. It wasn't the right time until now, and once again Mom was right; I'd know it when I saw it, and I did.

This sign was mine!

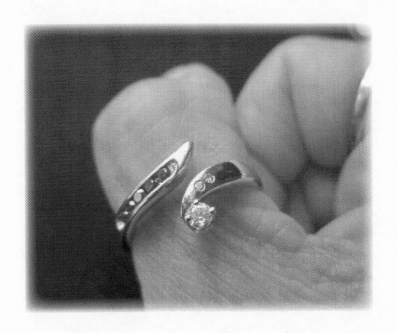

Epilogue

These powerful signs have weaved their infinite thread upon and through my life. They continue to do so almost daily, never failing to lift my spirit.

My sole requirement is to travel with my mind, heart, and eyes open. When I pay attention, most days, images of a heart will appear somewhere before me. I've only shared a few with you in this book.

I now recognize these shapes as my personal signs, they are reminders to me of an ethereal love, and even if only for a few seconds, I acknowledge the sign, share it if someone is with me, and most importantly to feel it. I ponder what I was thinking at the time of the heart sighting. Then I take a deep breath and remember to feel grateful for everything in my life, because I believe there is a reason for all of it. The Universe has the timing perfected. This has been proven to me! The journey isn't always an easy one, but we're not alone.

Before, "This Sign Was Mine" I found it tough to trust and not judge or try to control the situation(s) when I didn't know or understand the outcome. It was a more difficult task to *believe* that the mystery puzzle of my life was piece by piece being put in its proper place and then presented to me through signs, but that's what happened. I've learned to trust and to believe. Are you ready for your *signs*?

Have you discovered or thought about your Universal signs, God Winks, or reminders? If you want to explore the possibilities as I did, create a short list of the most monumental heart-felt, life changing moments as you remember them. What were the events and their timing? What people have left an impact on your life, either by coming into, or by leaving? Have you experienced any déjà vu moments, or premonitions?

Warning: The above practice could lead to the writing of your own unsuspected book or memoir.

About the Author

Patti Rae Fletcher was born and raised in the Detroit metro area. She loves the city with all of the wonderful diverse entertainment it has to offer. When life is chaotic and it's time for a break Patti enjoys being by the water, fishing, camping, hiking, gardening, writing poetry, reading, and relaxing to the sound of a crackling fire.

She credits her fifteen years of being employed in a school library as the key that turned her love of reading and literature into the passion she now has for writing.

Since 2004 she has studied writing technique through college courses and conferences. Before her book, (This Sign Was Mine), she published articles and photographs in over two dozen magazines. She has done work for Tangerine Press, (part of Scholastic) and also for Reading Town U.S.A.

Printed in the United States
By Bookmasters